RULE® is a Registered Service Mark of Karl R. Zimmer III
© 2017 Karl R. Zimmer III All Rights Reserved

This book is dedicated to all the girls and boys, old and young, who have ever been bullied, struggled with a learning disability or had trouble concentrating, felt inadequate or unworthy, or anyone who, in any way and for whatever reason has ever felt "not good enough."

The Boy who grew up to RULE® the WORLD
& how You can too!

This is the story about a boy. It could just as easily be about a girl, but this story is about a boy. Johnny Carlson was born in a big city, New York City, in the borough of Queens. As Johnny was to learn, his family would move quite often, and because of the many times the boy moved during his early years, he would find it hard to make friends. As soon as he made a new friend, the family would move, so he never felt it was easy to make and keep friends. He wouldn't realize it for many years, especially as difficult as his life would seem to be, but he was going to grow up to RULE® the world.

"Any kid, whether born in a big city, a little town, or out in the countryside, can learn to RULE® the world."

Soon after he was born, Johnny, his older sister Kathy, and their parents moved away from the big city, not far away but to a small community farther out on Long Island, called Syosset. Johnny and Kathy would play in their sand box, an old row boat their dad had filled with sand. Their two pets would run around the yard and play. Everything seemed joyful. Their parents had many friends who would visit from the big city and play with Johnny and Kathy and the pets. Almost before Johnny knew it, the family had to move again. This time it would be to a faraway land across the Atlantic Ocean, a country called Denmark. As difficult as all the moving was to be, and though Johnny didn't know it, he would grow up to RULE® the world.

"Kids can teach grown-ups that playing is not just about having fun, it is also a really important part of living a full life."

The trip to their new home across the ocean began on a ship. It was exciting to be on a ship, on the Atlantic Ocean, off to a faraway land. During their first night at sea, Johnny was startled awake by a loud crashing sound of ripping metal and the shrill of the emergency bells and sirens. His family rushed up on deck in case they had to get in the life boats, and Johnny could see all the deckhands running around, seemingly to nowhere. A part of him was scared, and yet there was another part of him that sensed everything was going to be okay. Sure enough, the ship he was on, the Stockholm, was able to limp back to New York Harbor. Though many lives were saved, the other ship, the Andrea Doria, sank in the wee hours of the following morning. With all that had already happened in Johnny's young life, he certainly didn't realize it yet, but he was growing up to RULE® the world.

"Sometimes, scary things happen, but you always have the power to make any day a great day."

After less than two years in Denmark, where Johnny learned to ride a bicycle and roller skate while he was just three years old, the family moved again, this time to Holland, also known as the Netherlands. Johnny would have to learn another language and another culture, and he wasn't even five years old, yet. It was hard for Johnny to make friends because he never knew when he'd have to move again, and Johnny was always different from the other kids. When he was in Denmark, he was the shy little American boy. Now in the Netherlands, he was the shy little American boy who spoke Danish and not Dutch. But Johnny learned to speak Dutch quickly and went to school where he made friends with Dutch kids and even became a little Dutch boy, himself. He was very good at roller skating, ice skating, throwing and kicking a ball, and even won the roller-skating championship for the entire school when he was only in the fourth grade. Johnny learned that even though he was not good at some things, he was very good at other things. Not everyone is good at the same things or at everything, but everyone is good at something. Johnny didn't know it yet, but he was growing up to RULE® the world.

"Even when you're not good at some things, you are really good at some other things."

Because Johnny had moved so much, and maybe because he was just different, he had trouble reading and writing, and he was teased and bullied by the older kids. One day, he was teased and bullied so much that three or four of his ribs got cracked while on the playground. It could have been because he was shy or different or because the other kids were jealous that he won the skating contest, but it taught Johnny that sometimes, some kids can be mean for no good reason. It wasn't just the kids that teased Johnny or were mean to him. When his dad would come home from a business trip, he'd quiz Johnny at the dinner table and then yell at Johnny for not answering a question quickly enough or especially if Johnny answered wrong. Johnny felt ashamed and even stupid because of the way his dad yelled at him. Johnny was a very sensitive boy and decided that maybe if he didn't speak, his dad wouldn't have reason to yell at him anymore. He also thought it would be best to hide his emotions and not show how sad or angry he was so that others wouldn't tease him. Johnny didn't realize it yet, but despite everything he was going through, he was growing up and learning how to RULE® the world.

"Even if someone is mean to you, you can still be strong and choose to be kind."

Johnny really liked living in the Netherlands, had made some good friends, and came to love Indonesian food, but now Johnny's family had to move again, and once again, it was across the ocean. Johnny was moving back to New York because his father got a promotion. Once again, Johnny had to leave all his friends, which made him very sad. Johnny had been growing up like a Dutch boy, and now he was going to have to make new friends and learn to read and write in a new language. You see, even though Johnny had been born in America and was going to be in the fifth grade, he wasn't quite 10 yet and would have to learn how to read and write English. Once again, Johnny was going to be different and the new kid. After the long journey across the Atlantic Ocean, as the ship sailed into New York Harbor, Johnny saw the Statue of Liberty in all her majesty. It was a beautiful sight and a powerful symbol of strength and freedom, and it gave Johnny hope for his new life. Though Johnny didn't know it yet, he was growing up to RULE® the world.

"Every girl and boy has the right to freedom and the pursuit of happiness."

Since Johnny had to learn how to read and write English, he attended a special English class. He felt as if he must not be smart because the other kids made fun of him. One time he had to read out loud in class and was so embarrassed because he didn't know words that were simple for the other kids. He tried really hard and went to the special class every school day. Johnny was good at riding his bicycle, running, and throwing a ball, and he was awarded a Gold Patch from the President's Council on Fitness, which made him feel proud. He was also made a member of the Safety Patrol to help the younger kids cross the busy street to the school. That made him feel important because he thought he was doing something meaningful. Feeling like he was growing up, Johnny announced to his parents, "I am not Johnny any more, now I am John." Even though he wasn't able to read that well, he believed he was good at some things, and that made him feel better about himself. John still didn't realize it yet, but he was growing up to RULE® the world.

"Being kind and of service to others, even when just helping them cross the road safely, is respectful and important."

John could hardly believe it, but his family had to move again, and he hadn't even been in his new house or new school one year! This time, they were moving far away to the middle of the country. His friends told John it was dangerous out there because of the gangsters in Chicago and the Indians they thought were still roaming the land called Indiana. Of course, they were wrong, but John believed what his friends told him. John just knew he was having to leave his friends, would have to make new friends, and even though he wouldn't have to learn a new language this time, he would be the new kid and different, again. Once his family moved to their new house, John learned that Indianapolis was famous around the world for a big car race called the Indy 500, he never saw any gangsters, and the only "Indians" running around were the kids in the new neighborhood playing "Cowboys and Indians." Sometimes, they would let John be an Indian, which he loved because he thought the Indians were really cool and special. He had even read books about the different tribes around the United States and wondered what they were really like. With everything they had been put through, they always respected the land and stayed true to their culture. You see, John didn't know it yet, but he really was growing up and learning how to RULE® the world.

"Every town is somebody's hometown. It may be far away, but it can be a wonderful, safe, and exciting place."

Not another year had gone by and John's family moved again. This time it was to the other side of the city, but it meant a new school and new friends. John hated moving. It was so hard to make new friends and to leave old ones. But John was just a kid and he had to do what his parents said, so he did the best he could. John was still struggling with reading and writing English, after all, he had learned how just a few years before, but he was now in the 8th Grade. His parents had put him in a private school with smaller classrooms so that he could get more attention from teachers and learn how to study. It was a big change from his other school. One day in class, he made a spelling mistake, and the teacher, Mr. Wiggle, yelled at him in front of the whole class. Mr. Wiggle, in a very loud and proper voice, yelled, "Carlson, your spelling is impoverished!" John didn't know what "impoverished" meant, but he knew it wasn't good. He felt so small and turned bright red with embarrassment, and he wished he could melt into the desk. Soon after, Mr. Wiggle left the classroom for a moment, and Matt, one of John's new friends looked over at him and said, "John, you can be King, and I'll be Vice-King," which made John feel ten feet tall. Maybe Matt knew that John was growing up to RULE® the world, but John still had no idea.

"Even when adults are mean, they can teach us that respect and kindness are always best. You are okay, no matter what anyone else says or does."

John was still struggling with his reading and writing, but he had met some really nice kids who seemed to like him, like Matt in English class, and that helped him feel better about himself. Even though John was thin and had been teased for being scrawny, he was very good at ice hockey and won awards for Most Valuable Player and Leading Scorer. In the new private school, he played soccer, which to him was easy because he had played that since he was very young in Denmark and the Netherlands. John earned a Varsity letter in soccer his very first year playing on the varsity team. All the teachers and coaches, and even the older kids were impressed with how good John was, and that made him feel really proud. Even though he wasn't good at reading and writing, though he was getting better, he realized he was very good at some things, especially those things he enjoyed. John didn't know it yet, but he was beginning to learn how to RULE® the world.

"Everybody deserves a chance to shine at something they do well."

John was shy, not only because he had been teased and bullied, but also for having been criticized so many times by his father. John had begun to play the drums in a little band with kids from the old neighborhood, but that was so far away that his parents and the other boys' parents didn't want to drive any of them to practice. John loved playing, though, and he saved some money and bought a drum-set at a pawn shop his dad had heard about. John set up the new kit in the basement and played to records he'd listen to through headphones. He could only play when nobody was home because the drums were so loud, but it was John's escape, a way for him to be alone and to have fun, so he didn't mind. It was also a way for him to express himself and to burn off some energy. During one summer, John washed dishes at a neighborhood, family restaurant, and he made enough money that summer to buy a used motorcycle, which would be his transportation to school as soon as he got his driver's license. A couple of his new friends played guitar, and the three of them formed a rock band. With practice, they got good enough to play at neighborhood parties and later played at a popular teen club, their school, and even a hotel. By exploring new records and learning how to play in front of other people, including adults, John was actually learning how to RULE® the world. He still didn't know it yet.

"You can find joy and happiness, even in the strangest places and at the silliest times. Enjoy every moment of every day."

The summer after graduating from High School, there was a terrible car accident. Two of John's good friends, including one of his best friends who played guitar in the rock band with John, did not survive. It was such a hard lesson for John and his friends to learn, that one day you can be playing with your buddies, and the very next day they might be gone. John had learned that lesson in a different way before because of all the times he and his family had moved, but that summer, losing Doug and Mark the way he did, was so hard. John was very sad for a long time. He would never forget his friends or the date of the accident, and he would carry that lesson with him, always. Every moment of every day is a moment to cherish, because every moment is precious. It can only be lived once, and then it is a memory. Though John didn't realize it yet, he really was learning how to RULE® the world.

"Life is precious, and friends live in our hearts long after they are gone. Love yourself and others, and everything you do."

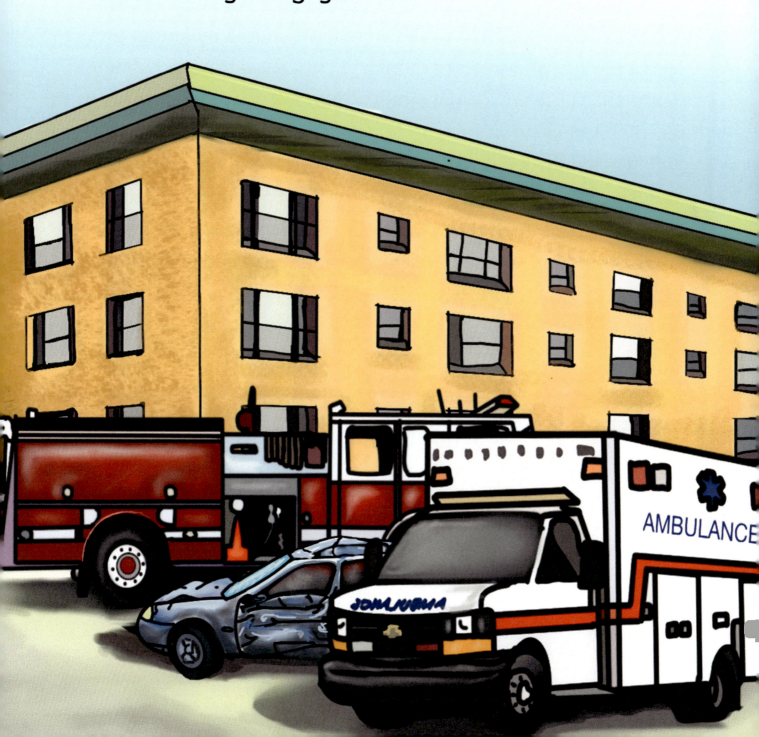

Before the end of that summer, John drove in his little MG, loaded to the fullest with clothes and his prized stereo speakers, which took up more than half of all the room in the car, and he set out for the great Northwest for college. He stopped in Portland, Oregon, to stay with his friend, Henry, who would be going to the same college in Tacoma, Washington. Once at the college, they decided to pledge a fraternity, and so his next adventure began. This would be a time of growth because John would have to make his own decisions. His parents were more than 2,000 miles away, and a phone call was too expensive. This was a time to begin to learn about life and responsibility. John felt all alone in many ways, partly because he was so shy, but he also knew that he was the only one who could decide what he wanted to be and how he wanted to live his life, and this was the time for him to figure that out. From the balcony of the fraternity house, he could see Mount Rainier in all its grandeur, and he realized that the world and everything it had to offer was out there, waiting for him. As much as he tried to make good decisions, he knew that he might make some mistakes along the way, but that was part of learning and growing. He could only do the best he could. He didn't know it yet, but he was learning, more and more, how to RULE® the world.

"We may be small compared to a giant mountain, but we can still make a big difference in the world, when we follow our dreams."

John came home for the summer and worked building houses. John pounded nails into wood, putting up walls and laying floors and roofs. He worked long hours in the hot sun, and he learned a great deal about hard work and working with different people. His foreman reminded John of his father, because he was very strict and yelled a lot. John learned that it was best to not say much and to do his work perfectly. The foreman knew John wanted to be an architect, and since he didn't like architects, he told John he was only good enough to sweep the floors, which was mean and not true. Not everyone likes the same things that we do, but they still deserve to be treated with respect. John did his best to not let what the foreman said bother him, because what the foreman or anyone else thought didn't change who John was. John realized that what mattered most was that he knew what was important and right for himself, and for him to work hard and respect others. John left university and took a year off to work, not really because he wanted to, but because he didn't know what else to do. He was struggling with many emotions, and nobody could help him, especially because he didn't understand what he was going through, himself. John worked as a tree trimmer and had to climb huge trees and cut branches away from power lines. The work could be dangerous, but John had always loved climbing trees as a young boy, and now he got to do it and get paid. John was learning new skills and he was learning a lot about himself and others. John was, indeed, learning how to RULE® the world, even though he didn't realize it, yet.

"No matter what you do,
do it the best that you can."

John was accepted at a university in the Desert Southwest. He moved to Albuquerque and lived with his good friend, Kevin. They had been friends since 7th grade, and Kevin had been going to university there for two years, already. It was great to have a friendly face in such a new and interesting place. John grew to love the Southwest, and he would spend all his free time driving around exploring the land of the Hopi, Navajo, and Apache around New Mexico and Arizona. When John first moved back from Europe, he had read books about the Indians and was fascinated by their spirit and strength. He learned even more, now, about how they lived, and he fell in love with the jewelry and culture of the Indians, the original Americans. While at class one day, one of John's architecture professors talked about how difficult it was to make a living as an architect, and John wondered if he really wanted to be an architect, or was it only a childhood dream?

"There is so much beauty in the world, and all you have to do is look for it."

He had also always wanted to fly airplanes and was interested in psychology, though his parents had discouraged him from pursuing that field, so he talked with a Navy recruiter about becoming a pilot. After taking some tests, the recruiter told him he could qualify but he'd have to go through a lot of training each summer and then, even after all that training and graduating from university, he would have to stay in the Navy more than six additional years. That added up to nearly 10 years, about half of his life so far, which seemed like such a long time and scared John, so he decided to go home for the summer to work and to talk with his parents. Part of him felt he was just treading water, not knowing what was best for him to do. John was, even more and more, learning about himself, about other people, and how to RULE® the world, yet he had no idea that he was learning anything at all.

"Follow your dreams no matter what anyone else says. When opportunity presents itself, let your dreams take flight."

Having worked very physical jobs every summer, John asked his parents if they would help him find a job where he could use his mind. John's mom thought it might be good for him to work at the family business, and John's dad said he could come down to the company with him and talk with the head of accounting to see if there was anything John could do there to help. That summer, John was given several different jobs around the company. In accounting, he learned all about costs and how to use a 10-key adding machine to tabulate pages and pages of numbers that he had to make sure were absolutely right. In the production department, he learned about and helped with scheduling, mounting printing plates for the big printing presses, and mixing special coatings used by the coating machines. He worked in the quality control laboratory where he learned how to run tests on paper and coatings to make sure they were exactly as they were supposed to be for the very demanding and specific uses required by the company's customers. After all, the company made materials used to wrap a variety of food items like ice cream sandwiches, "ice cream on a stick," as well as for butter and margarine. They also made "sticky paper" used to make special labels and trading cards. John loved what he was learning and felt he was making a difference by helping people with their jobs, and he was making his father proud.

"The best way to figure out what you are good at and what you enjoy is to do as many different things as you can."

John realized that as hard as his father had been on him, it was because he loved John and wanted the best for him. It was not easy being the "boss's son," but John did the best he could and listened more than he spoke. He knew he could learn much more by listening than he could by talking. John had learned so much and was doing such a good job that he was assigned to install the company's very first computer. Even though John wasn't making much money, he wanted to be responsible and live on his own, so he got an apartment, worked at the company during the day, and went to university at night. It was really hard, but he thought it was the right thing to do. You see, John really was learning how to RULE® the world.

Do you think he knew that, yet?

No, he sure didn't.

The years passed by. John had gotten married, had two beautiful children, and worked his way all the way up to the head of the company as President. He had worked very hard and helped the company grow into a leader in its field. As hard as he had worked, the hardest part of all was the travel and all the hours and days away from his family. John felt that maybe there was something else, something more important that he should be doing. He knew he had done a great job and had helped a lot of families in many ways, but he still felt that something was missing.

"Seeing the innocence of our children can teach us the true meaning of Love."

One day, while at his desk, a piece of paper appeared in the midst of the day's mail. On it were typed these words:

> "For every man there comes that special moment when he is physically tapped on the shoulder and offered the chance to do a very special thing - unique to him and fitted to his talents. What a tragedy if that moment finds him unprepared or unqualified for the work which would be his finest hour."
> Unknown

John knew in that moment that it was a message from above, from a powerful and divine being, Jesus.... It seemed impossible to John that Jesus would talk to him, directly. John didn't grow up in a religious family, and yet, John knew that it was an answer to what he had been asking,

"Is this really what I am here on Earth to do?"

Since his question had been answered by Jesus, John felt overwhelmed and humbled.

"Who am I to deserve this?" he asked.

Immediately a voice came back with the answer,

"Because you are me."

John couldn't believe what was happening, but he knew that whatever it was, it was powerful and meant for him in that moment. He also sensed that he was beginning to learn how to RULE® the world. We know it was more than the beginning, but John would realize that, only later.

"We all have a wise guide who is with us, always. Learn to listen to that guidance, and you will find joy and meaning in life."

Many years passed from the time Jesus came to visit John on that day. Through all that John had experienced in his life, all the moving and living in different countries, being bullied, struggling with a learning disability and low self-esteem, and always being different, John realized that by being true to himself and to all that he had learned from the time he was a very little boy, his greatest gift was already inside of him. He learned that all of us, every boy and every girl, have everything inside of us already to be anything we want to be. We are all born with the most powerful force in the Universe, and that is Love. John learned that everyone has a wise guide, like Jesus was for him, who is always present with pure love and support.

John learned that everyone he met along the way, every girl and boy, every teacher and coach, every mom and dad, every clerk at every store and every person of every color and every shape was much more like him than different. Every one of them wanted to be loved, wanted to be respected and to be understood, and every one of them wanted to have a life they could enjoy. Everyone wanted their children, if they were lucky enough to have them, to grow up to be respected, understood, and loved, and to live a life they could enjoy. By going through everything that John did, he grew up and learned how to RULE® the world; to Respect, to Understand, to Love, and to Enjoy the world and everyone who lived on it no matter what they looked like.

"Every boy and every girl, and that means you, already have everything you need, inside of you, to grow up to RULE® the world. All you have to do is to believe that you can. I believe in you."

What John was being asked to do by God and Jesus, was to teach others, every girl and boy, and every man and woman, that they, too, have everything they need, inside of them, already. You too, can RULE® the world.

- *Respect yourself as well as the feelings, opinions, beliefs, and cultures of others.*
- *Understand that others have feelings, opinions, beliefs, and cultures as real to them as yours are to you.*
- *Love yourself and others and everything you do.*
- *Enjoy each moment of every single day.*

You are loved and you are good enough, just the way you are. How cool is that!?

About the Author

Karl Zimmer III is an author, speaker, father, community leader, and successful CEO, who is sharing his story and teaching others how to RULE® the World. Karl moved many times while growing up, was bullied at school, and struggled with a learning disability. His journey has taught him that he had everything he needed, inside of him already, to make his life a good life, one worth living. Karl is sharing his story to help others who may be struggling like he did.

For questions, comments, or to learn more, visit: RULEtheWorldBooks.com
To arrange for Karl to speak at your event, write: books@iruletheworld.com

Made in the USA
San Bernardino, CA
14 January 2018